IONA

IONA

POEMS

Kenneth C Steven

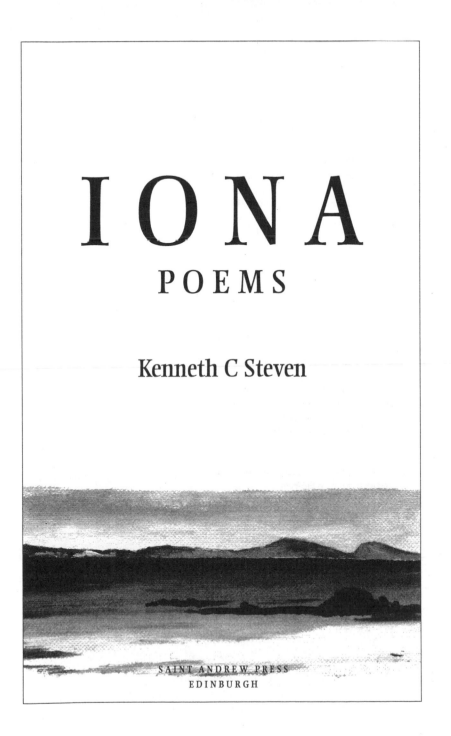

SAINT ANDREW PRESS

EDINBURGH

First published in 2000 by
SAINT ANDREW PRESS
121 George Street, Edinburgh EH2 4YN

Reprinted with amendment 2001, 2003, 2006

Copyright © Kenneth C. Steven 2000

10-digit ISBN 0 7152 0778 4
13-digit ISBN 978 0 7152 0778 9

British Library Cataloguing in Publication Data
A catalogue record for this book
is available from the British Library

Book design by Mark Blackadder.

Printed and bound by Bell & Bain Ltd., Glasgow

Contents

Poems in this collection previously appeared in:

Eclipse,
Edinburgh Review,
The Fireside Book,
The Herald,
Life & Work,
New Writing Scotland,
Nomad,
Northwords,
New Welsh Review,
Oasis,
Other Poetry,
Orbis,
Poetry and Audience,
Poetry Wales,
The Scots Magazine,
South,
Writing in Education Journal,
Weyfarers and
The Yorkshire Journal.

ESPECIALLY REMEMBERING THE
FOUR YOUNG MEN OF IONA WHO LOST THEIR LIVES
ON 13 DECEMBER 1998, AND FOR THE ISLAND
COMMUNITY AS THEY LOOK TO THE FUTURE
IN THIS NEW MILLENNIUM

A Lark

A handful of lark
Buoyant on the strings of a summer morning
Twirling and spinning songs
Overtures and symphonies
Though it has learned no music
In the schools of London or Paris
But is sight-reading instead
The kettledrums of the Atlantic
The white bells of the orchids
The violins of the wind.

Fire

Through the blurred lens of memory
I see a man
Cutting peats on the bare moon of a moorland.

All the stones that build his world are Gaelic:
Fishing, mending, stories, singing, prayers –
London's out of touch, a blurred voice on the radio.

All day his back bends and the blade shapes
Drenched, dark wedges of peat
That are stacked to dry in the long summer wind.

Inside each slab the ferns of Culloden, of clearance,
Of the battle to evict starvation –
Imprints of history like fossils.

This is the peat that lights the memory,
That fires the struggle,
That keeps the heart burning.

Garve

They have all blown away,
The ones who knew these hills by name,
Who translated the wind, who spoke
The same language as the curlew.

I remember
The day I came here in childhood
To watch the last of my mother's people buried
Under a weight of memories and snow.

They are replaced by foreign bodies
With Range Rovers and mobile phones,
Who smooth the road to London in a day
And do not care.

The Small Giant

The otter is ninety percent water
Ten percent God.

This is a mastery
We have not fathomed in a million years.

I saw one once, off the teeth of western Scotland,
Playing games with the Atlantic –

Three feet of gymnastics
Taking on an ocean.

Agates

After battling the shore
An April morning, you find them sometimes
Embedded in the shingle.

Tumbled by the Atlantic
Luminous globes of stones
All coloured – orange and green and blue.

Once upon a time, when the islands belched
Like angry dragons with volcano
Agates were left in the lava.

See-through bubbles –
Ringed like beautiful Saturns –
Danced up from the tide in shining.

Cannich

On a June day the air is warm to breathe
Even here, seven miles from anywhere
In the middle of the moors. The loch
Is blue and placid as an eye. Across its glass
A lace dragonfly patters the air, living threads
Sewn into wings; a heron gets up ungainly from the shore,
And lumbers heavily away.
I leave my clothes in a tangle, run out onto a ledge
And land in melted ice. Cold grips like a fist,
Hurts the middle of the heart, crushes;
I scrabble and splash, fight and bless
This sheer delicious pain. Yet slowly, slowly,
I grow into the cold, turn warm with numbness.
I tread water, listen in the middle of this gem
To buzzards mewing in the pool of sky, to six doves
Racketing from cover across the light.
I swim out, soundless as a trout,
And plash across the rocks, dripping millions of diamonds.

Waterland

The flat land is under water. All night
Rain slashed from a low sky
Till the yard sang and shone with black wetness.
Three times I listened at the window,
Hearing the river's deep gash through the hills,
The little serpent streams that wove the fields –
The whole world under water.

This morning I went out and the skies rolled back
Like giant white rugs. A bleary eye of sun
Opened far east and welled into our land
So ten thousand bits of water came alive,
Turned to silver mirrors and I heard the geese
Rising in acres, crying across the light.

Scalpay

In the midst of the mess of Edinburgh
With the languages round me
Babbling like some demented radio
I think of Scalpay, that granite boulder off the coast of Harris
Today when the bridge to it will be opened.
I remember going there last year
From the lunar eeriness of Harris
To houses like clams crowded round shores,
Loud flocks of children laughing in Gaelic,
Boats spilling fish onto a sunlit pier.
I told someone I was a friend of Finlay MacSween's;
At once I was whirled away to tea and stories and questions,
Given a whole salmon from a ferryman's freezer,
As many greetings as I could remember to take home with me.
I left that island with more kindness
Than I ever carried in my life before,
Yet I remember seeing the first black lumps of bridge as I went
Sprouting from the opposite headlands
And fearing that when I came back again
A whole world, older and wiser,
Would be lost and gone forever.

Now and Then

The old ones read the land and the sea like books;
They understood the skies, they listened to the rain,
They did what the winter told them.

Now almost all of them have gone;
Those that are left glint like the odd gold grain
Swirled from a stream – rare and precious.

Carsaig

Over the edge of the moon of Mull
The talons of cliff sink into the sea.

Down below beneath the eagles
This is almost a strange Pacific.

Dripping red flowers, birdsong, ferns
In a jewellery of falls and pools.

Bees weaving their own song
In a golden cage of sunlight.

This Eden sleeping strange and rich
In the grey wolf of the Atlantic.

Scurdie Ness

Where the geese rise in long
Slow arrowheads, where the winter sun
Strikes like flint at the low hills.
Where the sea scars in from Norway,
Sharp and colder than snow.

All afternoon we crabbed about that headland
Looking for agates, searching through the stones
For little bits of pink and white with rings.
Out on the edge of the sea a ship fought south;
The cormorants gathered in covens on the rocks.

We came back against the wind, hands raw
Like fleshless bone. The sun sank into flames of cloud
And in a shudder the whole of Fife
Was wintered. Our pockets rattled with knuckles of agate
As the first snow petalled across the hills.

Logie

When I was a boy I went every Saturday
To the north end of the island –
To her farmhouse for eggs.

I walked against the wind
That was full of snowflakes
The salt knife of the sea.

When I got to her doorway
The collies flowed out at me
Black and white bounces of barking.

She brought me into her home
Gave me six eggs in a box
To take back for the coming week.

Last night her son was drowned
Returning in a boat at midnight
He was lost and will not come home.

The Row

There is a kettle on the range
With its lid rattling and foaming –
The kitchen smells of butter and new meat.
The dog lies fanned out on the floor,
Mild eyes the colour of whisky, watching,
Me shivering on an ancient chair,
My hair hedgehogged and shining with water,
Ten years old, having fallen in a bog.

Outside the night has come down
Like tar. There is only one rickety lane
Riding away west, and that has been swallowed.
All has slid into dark except a few flint bits of star
That spark the skies.

And I am shivering on the kitchen chair,
Watching the mellow blinking of the collie's eyes,
Ten years old, waiting and waiting for the row.

Resolution

And suddenly the sun broke through the sky
And I was home, a broad Atlantic
Stumbled over rocks and creamed in rage
A tug of storm hung low across the shores
Water colour blue and broken green.

How did I lose my way or once believe
That there were riches bigger than this simplicity
Or that any other tide could speak, or heal
The wounds of searching deeper cut than pain
Where here I stood by heaven hearing God?

Lamb

I found a lamb
Tugged by the guyropes of the wind
Trying so hard to get up.

It was no more than a trembling bundle
A bag of bones and wet wool
A voice made of crying, like a child's.

What a beginning, what a fall,
To be born on the edge of the world
Between the sea and America.

Lamb, out of this island of stone
Yellow is coming, golden promises,
The buttery sunlight of spring.

Iona

Is this place really nearer to God?
Is the wall thin between our whispers
And his listening? I only know
The world grows less and less –
Here what matters is conquering the wind,
Coming home dryshod, getting the fire lit.
I am not sure whether there is no time here
Or more time, whether the light is stronger
Or just easier to see. That is why
I keep returning, thirsty, to this place
That is older than my understanding,
Younger than my broken spirit.

Storm

Today there is no going out;
We are shut in; Mull and Jura and Ireland
Have been taken by storm, the wind
Rushes through lofts like a demented housewife.

Suddenly all colours have been abolished,
Made illegal overnight. The sea has lost its head,
Comes in longships across the headlands
Raping and pillaging without mercy.

Tomorrow when all this is over,
Green stones will lie flicked up from the storm
On Columba's Bay. Bits of sky will break open
To blue lagoons.

Edge

If you come here in summer
It is islands and islands as far west as America.
Sudden thunderings of cloud,
Light blessing the sea,
Orchids blowing across every moorland.
Sometimes a seal bumps off rocks;
The air is raucous and torn with birds.
Out on the edges of headlands, here and there,
Like chinks of gold, men and women
With Gaelic in their tongues –
Psalms in their voices.

The Death of Columba

In the morning he is gone.
Only the face is left, the eyes,
But their light has passed, departed
Into the place he trusted so much.

They come with orchids and wild irises –
The poor people – their bare feet sore
Over the hard stones. Their faces have melted,
Word has ripped through their world like a knife.

But the day comes nonetheless. A tangle of otters
Makes rings in the shallow blue of Port Ban.
A branch of eagle steers out across Ben More,
Sunlight blesses the cloister floors.

They carry him to his last sleep,
Each one remembering the pieces of his life
They knew. They lay him soft in the grave's dark;
A lark tells them to sing, to sing and not weep.

Hebrides

Staffa is an organ
Thrown overboard by giants long ago.

Jura is a beast with its head down, sleeping,
Its back volcanic, its winds eroded.

Tiree is a gust of fields and houses
Low in the water on the world's rim.

Lewis is a congregation of huddled sermons
Battened-down hatches in a mist of whisky.

Eigg is one milk tooth biting the sky
Searching thirstily among sagging clouds.

Islands

Even at midsummer the wind is always there:

A chasing sky, grass beaten flat,

Gulls bending through torn blue sky,

And somewhere a washing line flapping with clothes,

Thrashing the wind, as if waving

To all the ones who left these islands,

Who were blown overseas at the mercy of gales –

The storms of history –

And never returned.

The Giver of Life

I see a man coming towards me
Across the edge of the shore where light
Breaks and cries in an endless voice.
In one hand he carries water, fresh and clear
In the other earth, rich and crumbled.
Where he stoops in the pale shadow
He brings forth to the treeless land a sapling
Gently presses its roots in the soft ground.
Mingling the earth and water for its strength, he says:
This is the life I give you, for storm and calm,
For harvest and drought, for spring and winter,
Grow for the light of the world.

Christmas Eve

The farms shone out like cries
White in the mist. As always
I felt this was the bed of a place
That once had lain under water.

In every window the red glow
Of Christmas. Upstairs a child waiting
In the warm secrecy of the dark
For morning, that long-awaited morning.

I looked out across the vague grey of the river
And beyond was nothing, only the rushing of the roads,
Kingdoms away, worlds beyond this world –
This timeless and priceless home.

Prayer

If you do not believe in God
Go on a blue spring day across these fields:
Listen to the orchids, race the sea, scent the wind.

Come back and tell me it was all an accident
A collision of blind chance
In the empty hugeness of space.

The Potato Pickers

Hollows of mist; September smells so thick
Of chestnuts scudded down and leaves in wet
And water drumming choked towards the town.

Farms lie here, dark as blackened books
And dykes rib over chests of curving land
Into the rain.

Like fish creels crates are steepled
There by the field's edge. Slumped with mud
The tractor's rumbled track reflects the sky.

Now the pickers splay down in the ruts
Thudding their baskets with pale lumps
All out of shape and smooth as fossil shells.

They move like ragged crows across the day
Legs planted wide, heads slanted over rain
Until in bleary stars lights home the dusk.

The Changes

A peewit came
This spring to the island
In snowflakes, daffodils and the wind.

Usually a whole gale of them blow in,
Their voices like children's, their flight
Soft and dipping across the sea fields.

But this year
Only one came back
In the wild sunlight of March.

We watched and waited
We listened in the mornings
But there was just the one peewit.

Strange and hopeless
Up on the clay dark of the moorland
Calling and calling without end.

Barvas

A landscape battered flat by the wind;
Thistles wave their swords like Viking warriors,
Flowers hide under banks, their heads bowed.
Houses lie tousled along the roadside,
The skeletons of dead tractors and of vans
Stretching along the sparse, blown grass.
A long way west the sea combs in
Coral white, breaking on the rocks' teeth,
And the water is wolf-grey, not blue,
But pitiless, flint, the fist of the Atlantic.

The Search for Christ

At times you are distant
Turned away among cold stars
As hopeless to the sailor
As moonless reefs in storm.

Believe me, I have tried to find you
In the Bethlehems of poor sojourn
Seeking a miracle in the tenement homes
Of poverty and drunken dark.

Only among mountains beaten by cold
The blood dripping from a rowan branch
Have I felt the nails piercing my heart
And the voice of crucified love.

Highland

This land is cut to the bone
Ashamed of a sin it has not committed,
Lost in its own history.

A Presbyterian wind scours the hollows,
Searching anything that does not know repentance.

The burns weep for their iniquities,
Ask forgiveness through the torrent of winter.

The raven devils a blown sky,
Torn black rags of wings, gimlet sight,
Ready to peck the blue eyes of a lamb.

Only the rowan bends slender among the rocks,
A shingle of pale leaves, and every autumn,
Unafraid to break the Sabbath,
Shakes clutches of bright orange berries.

Old Woman

And so she ages by the day.
The threads that wove the fabric of her mind
Fray one by one and will not mend –
She is far away in her thoughts.

Once she was beautiful, and knew it;
Once her blood's fire burned in a man's veins
Night after night, and her colours
Enflamed the coals of his heart.

Who may see that now,
When the nurses bring her things and swear
Behind her back because she cannot hold
A spoon, or manage all the stairs?

Inside her yet, beneath the autumn-wrinkled face
She lies, the girl she was: the dreams, the dance, the light,
Not dead, but sleeping, still alive and clear
To those who know to look beneath the skin.

On the West Coast of Harris

I have seen them in my mind's eye
Ploughing these rocks for food
Year after year. They live here yet
Though they are dead; long before dawn
They are out at labour along this coast
Bent against wind and sea
Till the last blink of day, till they turn home
To dark rest. They did no evil
All their years, they steered by heaven,
And where was their reward except in bitter winter,
Clearance, grief? They are my fathers,
I carry them in my eyes,
Will not lose sight of them.
Now I come back to this land,
Easy, young, the world in my pocket,
And think still it is I who am poor,
And they the immeasurably rich.

A Little Miracle

Two black and brown puffs of duckling
Little bits of thistledown
That could have blown away in a breeze
Bobbing beneath the bank of the river.

As I approached they shot out into the current
Were washed away like flotsam
Making high peeps of sound
Till a bend snatched them from sight.

All night I worried for them
Went out into the raining darkness
To the lion roar of the river
Listened in hope for their peeping.

And I wondered that such little things survived at all,
Winter and spring, the angry traffic of this world,
To grow safe and strong into wings
To learn to fly.

The Birth

He is born, she whispered,
Go down and look at him.
Six in the morning and I said nothing,
Still woolly with dreams,
Buried in the room's warm darkness.
I struggled slowly into clothes,
Thudded down the wooden staircase.
Outside it was March, the land all scabbed and sore
With winter; the wind a rusty blade,
Cutting the eyebrows and the wrists,
The river whiskying away downstream and roaring
With snow and stories.
At the barn I opened a door into darkness,
Blinked in the thick, warm smell of hay.
A bit of wet sunlight broke through the window;
I saw the mother like a granite boulder –
Even her eyes exhausted –
That thin patch of lamb beside her,
Shivering. He tried to push up the sky from above him,

And his legs melted away like wax;
He cried a single time.
I went closer, on soft and reverent feet,
And this was suddenly a Bethlehem,
His voice a child's, as vulnerable as Christ's.

The Wild Raspberries

Outsprinted by the main road now
This lane disappears into nowhere –
Bearded by birds' nests in the springtime,
Hung thick with white and yellow flowers.
In August when the skies
Turn the blue of a rock pool, the wild raspberries
Ripen in hundreds by the broken wall.
I used to go there with a pail and deep boots,
Dunt down bits of fruit as the evening
Came blading from the west in bright gold.
Years ago, when the people thought they were rich
With wild harvest: petals of mushrooms,
Strong trout from the streams, hazelnuts and apples –
Young children would bleed their mouths
On these berries, hour after hour.
Now we think we are poor,
Yet no-one comes to pick the fruit
But leaves it to turn the colour of dark bruises
And die where it grew, as the juggernauts
War and rumble through our village streets.

Learan

Mid-afternoon and still the light
Blues this silent room. A few dried flowers
Blown out by the cold of winter
Dust the table. And in the window
Trees begin to break with green, their leaves
Uncurl and whisper in an edge of breeze.
This farm lies, a northern shell
A cut of grass between the rubbled Highland rocks
The eyes of lochs that stretch across the west:
It has survived the gales and stands
On wooden crutches, looking at the light
Begin to sink. The room falls in on shadow –
One by one our lights ignite the dark.

The Well

I found a well once
In the dark green heart of a wood

Where pigeons ruffled up into a skylight of branches
And disappeared.

The well was old, so mossed and broken
It was almost a part of the wood

Gone back to nature. Carefully, almost fearfully,
I looked down into its depths

And saw the lip of water shifting and tilting
Heard the music of dripping stones.

I stretched down, cupped a deep handful
Out of the winter darkness of its world

And drank. That water tasted of moss, of secrets,
Of ancient meetings, of laughter,

Of dark stone, of crystal –
It reached the roots of my being

Assuaged a whole summer of thirst.
I have been wandering for that water ever since.

October

All night she listens to the wind
Dreams of bumping her kite on the breeze.

She goes to school with a satchel on her back
And three acorns clutched in her hand.

She balances along the edge of a wall
And wonders how far away winter can be.

She sings a bit of song then watches a robin
Listens to the liquid gems of his voice.

She goes scruffling through piles of autumn leaves
Picks up a conker like a new –polished button.

She comes in late to the autumn classroom
Says she stopped to hear the raindrops singing.

Solway

In the evening boats come in
With torn-up scraps of gulls.
Their engines rub the silence, nudge the water,
Till fastened, they lie on their bellies
As the tide goes out to sea.
Their sailors climb aboard the land
The voices rise and fall along the road,
As some go in for drinks and others watch
As lemon-coloured lights swell out from windows of hotels.
Long across the bay is England
Lying still at anchor, far and blue.

A Poem for Ann

Three feet small
With dreams as big as Christmas.

A cornfield of curls
And a smile that would melt a soldier.

When you cry
All of you falls to pieces;
Everyone comes running to mend you.

At night your eyes look huge;
You are afraid of the owl
That ghosts your bedroom window.

I tell you a story
But you are kingdoms and princes away
Long before the ending.

In the morning I will bring you blackbirds
And put the sun on your pillow.
I will tie your laces,
And pray safe roads for your feet.

Sabbath

This dusk the sky's a single blue pane
The trees etched out of winter blackness.

The moon is a boy's balloon
Stuck up in the branches.

I go into the shadowed sanctuary of the church
Its air blessed by petals of candles.

I see the eyes, waxy in the light, watching,
Waiting, patient with the need of faith.

In these faces, ploughed by grief and struggle,
Are many roads to God.

Greatness

I met a little man from Glasgow
Who lives five flights above the city –
Disused sidings, empty factories and sheds,
The bitter dregs of drunken, late night youths.

But from his bedroom window he can see
On clear, blue days of winter
The single sharp crystal of Goat Fell
And the distant back of Ben Lomond.

The Abbey Fields

That night our feet scythed the long wet grass
Made a wandering furrow through the field
Towards the ponies. They loomed across to us
Their faces soft, their breath warm;
The black was furred with moths, the air airless.
The trees hung in eerie orange light
And somewhere on a hillside, behind farms and
                walls and roads
A fox kept yapping, his dry flat bark carrying
Across the long dark. South of us
The end of England pointing out into the sea
And the beginning of morning.

Service

Two nuns exchange welcomes;
Their soft words like the water
That flows through the cress at a well's mouth.

Candles melt in the darkness
Cover the Christ with light like sweat –
His wounds cry with new blood.

People's mouths pray
Their words gentle as grass, their eyes
Clenched with faith.

This is the Easter of life;
Waiting in the dark before dawn –
Trusting the sun.

Mushrooms

The night before a great moon full of honey
Had flowed up behind the hills and poured across the fields.

The leaves were rusting, the wheat whispered
Dry and gold in the wind's hands.

Andrew and I went to Foss. We drove over the hills
That were blustery with huge gusts of sunlight.

We stopped and walked to the loch, left two trails
Through the grass, came on the mushrooms by accident,

A village of strewn white hats
The folds of their gills underneath as soft as skin.

We almost did not want to take them, as if
It would be theft – wronging the hills, the trees, the grass.

But in the end we did, we picked them with reverence:
And they broke like bread between our hands,
         we carried them home,

Pieces of field, smelling of earth and autumn;
A thanksgiving, a blessing.

After the Rain

I woke at first light,
Listened to the quiet after long rainfall.

Like a strange resurrection
The clouds were torn, blown into pale shreds,
October above them blue and beautiful.
I went out, barefoot, found the meadows lying underwater,
The oaks still above their own reflections.

I waded out through white water,
Swayed back folds of still water,
As the swallows flickered in the morning air
And the Sabbath bells flowed over the valley.

I thought of Christ in the fields of Galilee,
His feet swathing through lilies and water,
Early in the birdsong of the morning.

The Stars

From the age of five my sight was smudged as a mole's;
I wore tortoiseshell-rimmed glasses that were
            never quite clean
And the stars looked white and indistinct
Vague pearls in a distant heaven.
On my fifteenth birthday my parents gave me lenses –
Little cupped things that drifted into sight across my irises.
Driving home with them that night I suddenly
            caught sight of something,
Got out by the edge of the field and looked,
Amazed and disbelieving as if Christ himself
            had healed my eyes,
For the stars were crackling and sparking
Like new-cut diamonds on the velvet of a jeweller's window,
So near and clear I could have stretched and held them
Carried them home in my own pocket.
That was the gift my parents gave me on my birthday –
The stars.

Snow Light

Yesterday I went into the silence
The snow cobwebs that hung in rafters
Icing the trees, scarving every gable end.

And I thought how strange and lucky
After Flanders, after Hiroshima, after Chernobyl,
This untroubled whiteness of winter
Still blessing the land like broken bread
From the hand of a forgotten God.